20

COMMUNICATION TIPS

FOR FAMILIES

Other books in the
20 Communication Tips Series:

20 Communication Tips for Couples
by Doyle Barnett

Forthcoming:
20 Communication Tips at Work
by Eric Maisel, Ph.D., and Marc Allen

⊚ INTRODUCTION ⊚

I remember the time I counseled my first family. I had counseled individuals and couples before, and I thought I had learned a thing or two. I was feeling pretty confident. How much harder could it be to counsel a family than to counsel a fighting couple, a mute teenager, or a depressed adult?

Plenty.

In walked five people: mom, dad, and their

three children. The youngest was a boy of six with the energy of a power station. Then came a boy of nine whose primary goal in life looked to be finding reasons to whack his brother. Then came the sister, all fifteen years of her, as ironic and distant as a human being could be. Last came mom and dad, who appeared to hate each other, if hate wasn't too mild a word.

They clearly didn't want to be there. Did I?

In my training as a psychotherapist, I was taught

20
COMMUNICATION TIPS
FOR FAMILIES

A 30-MINUTE GUIDE TO a BETTER FAMILY RELATIONSHIP

ERIC MAISEL, PH.D.

NEW WORLD LIBRARY
NOVATO, CALIFORNIA

New World Library
14 Pamaron Way • Novato, California • 94949
Copyright © 2000 by Eric Maisel, Ph.D.
Cover illustration: Kathy Warinner
Cover and text design: Mary Ann Casler
Editorial: Georgia Ann Hughes

Library of Congress Cataloging-in-Publication Data
Maisel, Eric, 1947–
20 communiation tips for families: a 30-minute guide to a better family relationship / Eric Maisel.
p. cm.
ISBN 1-57731-166-3 (perfect)
1. Communication in the family. 2. Interpersonal communication. 3. Family. I. Title: Twenty communication tips for families. II. Title.

HQ734 .M24 2000
646.7'8—dc21   99-086447

First Printing, April 2000   •   ISBN 1-57731-166-3
Printed in Canada on acid-free paper • Distributed by Publishers Group West

10 9 8 7 6 5 4 3 2 1

FOR ANN

☺ CONTENTS ☺

✿ FOREWORD ✿

The goal of this book is to help your family improve the way you communicate. In these pages you will find twenty tips that you can put into practice right away. These tips will let the love and generosity that exist in your family flow more freely and make your family life not only more pleasant but even joyous.

Families can be great places or they can be

miserable places. Too often, family members get caught up in their own worries and needs and haven't the patience or empathy to communicate with each other. They criticize, command, or lash out rather than love and cherish. Learning communication skills is vital because if you can just point out better ways for family members to be — say, kinder in the way they speak to each other — amazing growth and change can occur.

Only through speaking and listening — that is,

through effective communicating — can these miracles of improvement happen. So start today, and invite the rest of your family along. Use the love in your heart and what this book has to offer. Together they will make a tremendous difference in the life of your family.

All you have to do is try these tips, but please don't go it alone! Invite your whole family to read this book and involve themselves in the process of communicating more effectively and lovingly. It will only take about thirty minutes to read this slim book, and everybody in your family can make that small investment in the future of your communal life together. So pass this book around right at the start — or give each family member his or her own copy!

things, but nothing had prepared me for this. The session went as one might have expected it to go — scores of charges leveled, mom and dad venting, the kids cringing or making themselves absent, feelings getting hurt on all sides, and me wishing I were on a desert island, far away from people.

At the end of yet another assault — maybe mom had leveled a charge at dad, or vice versa, I cannot remember which — I finally blurted: "What is needed here is a little more generosity of spirit!"

This little outburst had the strangest effect. The family fell silent and everybody visibly softened. I perked up. Well! It looked like talking about things like love, kindness, and generosity, and not "problems," might be the route to family change. Here was something to think about!

For the past fifteen years I have counseled individuals, couples, and families. I now know that what I intuited in that first family session is the absolute truth. Family communication is possible, but love must be the lubricant. Until a person becomes a more feeling creature — which means feeling pain, anger, hurt, and disappointment sometimes, but also love, kindness, friendship, and generosity — a brick wall blocks genuine communication. So here is a bonus tip: feel. If you open up your heart, pain may spill out — but so will love. It is then that communicating will begin.

It would be great if people were effective, willing communicators. But most people aren't. The ability to communicate takes learning, practice, courage, patience, and a lot more. We have to be able to tolerate frustration, lower our defenses, recognize what we want to say, and then deliver our message in a clear, kind way. How many of us can do that well? Not very many. The problems that families have in communicating are exactly the same problems that people have in communicating, whether they are at work or at home, in Tokyo or in Topeka, and whether they're twelve, thirty-five, or sixty.

TIP 1

COMMUNICATION STARTS WITH YOU

There are no magic bullets that will turn an uncommunicative, oppositional, difficult, tense, or hostile family environment into a paradise of effective communication and good will. What there is to work with is the love that already exists, the hope in each family member's heart for something better, and the innate power of individual people to try harder, *beginning with you.* You can't ask your husband or wife, son or daughter, or father or mother to do a better job of communicating if you aren't striving to be an honest, effective listener and speaker. The ball is in your court.

Waiting for someone else in your family to begin communicating won't work. If you wait for your child to speak and say what is on her mind, she will probably continue keeping her fears, frustrations, and problems a secret forever. If you wait for your mate to start the communication ball rolling, you will have another long wait coming. If you keep dreaming about your parents airing their disagreements and coming to some happy resolution, probably that will remain a dream and not become a reality. If you yourself have something on your mind but can't find the right moment to bring it up, ask yourself when the right moment will be.

Accept the challenge. Become your family's first communication wizard.

EVERYBODY IN YOUR FAMILY HAS A DUTY
TO COMMUNICATE.
STILL, SOMEBODY HAS TO START.

TIP 2

THE FIRST RULE OF LOVE IS TO LISTEN

Often we don't want to hear what another person is saying because if we really listened, we would be obliged to take that person's feelings and needs seriously. But if you love the members of your family, you do want to take their feelings and needs seriously, and this means that you have an absolute duty to listen.

Loving listening goes far beyond accurately hearing another person's words, although that's the starting point. Because people feel vulnerable, they often say things in guarded or indirect ways. Or they say so many things in a single sentence that it's hard to identify the main point. Or they don't know what they have in mind — they say that their room is too hot, but they're really worried about failing algebra. It often takes a concerted effort to identify a person's real message. Loving listening is an important skill, and it takes time and practice to master.

Here is how to master loving listening:

1. Pay undivided attention when someone is speaking to you.

2. Be more interested in what is being said than in figuring out how to reply or fix the problem.

3. Wonder to yourself what is *really* going on. Use your powers of intuition and your lifetime of experience to understand what your child, mate, or sibling is getting at. Plus, you can ask questions!

4. Take the time to listen, to consider what's being said, to gain clarity, and to frame direct but loving responses. Communication takes *time* — and deserves the time it takes.

©

YOU WILL BE AMAZED BY HOW MUCH
MORE LOVE THERE IS IN
YOUR FAMILY IF YOU AND OTHER FAMILY
MEMBERS JUST LISTEN.

TIP 3

SHARE YOUR THOUGHTS AND YOUR FEELINGS

We don't like to admit to ourselves that we are sad, disappointed, angry, upset, or that we have any negative feelings whatsoever. We especially don't like to admit such things to another person. Maybe we fear reprisals, or feel that there is no hope of anything changing, or suspect that we will make matters worse by communicating our real feelings.

But communicating your feelings is vital! It is the only way to tell the truth and often the only way to start making things better.

Say that you are bothered by your mate's spending habits. You think that his motorcycle hobby or her doll collection is taking up too much family money. You may think you are expressing your thoughts and feelings when you say something like: "You know, we don't really have enough money for another doll, even if it is going to increase in value. We need that money right now!" The following types of statements are both more thoughtful and express more of your core feelings:

- "I'm really disappointed that we have such different ideas about how to spend money. We have a problem that we've got to address."

- or -

- "I'm really scared how we're living from paycheck to paycheck. It's stressing me out that we have no savings. I've really got to talk about my stress level and what we can do about it."

Such responses open doors. They're invitations to solve problems at the core. Once family members begin to communicate this way, they'll never want to speak from their heads again. Then your family will be communicating with heart.

IF A MESSAGE IS JUST AN IDEA, IT WASN'T SENT BY A HUMAN BEING. ALL HUMAN MESSAGES HAVE FEELINGS ATTACHED.

TIP 4

TAKE HEART —
FAMILY COMMUNICATING
ONLY FEELS
IMPOSSIBLE

Sometimes family gatherings are so tense that it feels like everyone is at war with everyone else. Maybe Mom just made a casual but slightly cruel remark about Sally's hair. Dad is upset that he's been outvoted about what pizza to order. Johnny is still stewing about his English grade, which has nothing to do with anyone at the table but which nevertheless renders him mute and uncommunicative. Put this all together and you have a recipe for a miserable time and a missed opportunity to enjoy one another's company.

This happens so often, in so many situations, that parents and children begin to think that actual communication is just a myth. It isn't. Any family can do a better job of communicating and living well together. Sometimes this takes major changes, but more often it just takes practicing simple skills and paying better attention to what people in the family are thinking and feeling. Usually, if even one person in the family sets out to improve family communication, the whole family is encouraged and more loving communication can begin.

You may be in a family where somebody is a communication enemy. Maybe he or she is an alcoholic, a philanderer, or is living some other big lie that he or she refuses to divulge. These circumstances are the most serious obstacles to effective family communication, especially when the whole family colludes in not speaking about the alcoholism or the philandering. But even here, if at least one family member will break the code of silence, then positive change, new intimacy, and better relating can begin.

◎

TAKE HEART. ALMOST ANY FAMILY —
YOURS INCLUDED — CAN LEARN TO
COMMUNICATE BETTER!

TIP 5

BE DIRECT —
BUT KIND

It is important to be able to say things directly, in short, simple, clear sentences. When you say things indirectly or at great length, that usually means that you feel you don't have a leg to stand on, you are ambivalent about your message, or you hope the person you are talking to won't discover your secret agenda. It is better to be clear before you speak, know what you want to say, trust that you have the right to communicate, and then deliver your message simply and directly.

Here are some examples of clear, direct speaking.

• "You've been spending a lot of extra time at work. Does that mean that we have a problem?"

• "You seem to have much less homework this year than last year. Is that right? Or are you less motivated this year?"

• "I want to stop working and start a home business. I know that has a lot of ramifications, but I'd like us to talk about it."

- "We've been having sex pretty infrequently. I wonder what's up?"

- "You and your sister have been fighting a lot recently. I wonder what we can do about that?"

- "I feel like we need a vacation but I also know that we don't have any money put aside. Can we talk about some vacation options?"

Being direct isn't the same as being blunt or mean. Always leave room for kindness in the spaces between words. By your tone, your inflection, your body language, and by the words themselves, you can communicate the fact that you have something to say but that you don't mean to hurt, insult, or criticize your listener. If you pay attention to both sides of the equation — both to directness and to kindness — you will grow stronger as a communicator and also invite more love into every family interaction.

ALWAYS SPEAK LOVINGLY,
NOT JUDGMENTALLY.

TIP 6

NEVER SEND MIXED MESSAGES

A mixed message is a message in which two contradictory ideas are blithely — and often bizarrely — conjoined. Here are some classic mixed messages:

- "Please get all of your homework done and get to bed early."

- "I really want to have sex with you tonight, but I'm just not in the mood."

- "Grandpa, I'd love to visit you over spring

vacation, but I've only got a week off."

• "My job is killing me. By the way, I've asked to take on a couple of new assignments."

• "Mom, I really think we should eat healthier meals, but can we have hamburgers and fries tonight?"

If you said to your son, "I want you to do all of your homework, no matter how long it takes, but I also want you to go to bed early, no matter what," you and your son would both have to laugh at the absurdity and logical impossibility of what you're demanding. But we often do want to make illogical and impossible demands on other people, so we cut and paste our messages to make a single message that almost makes sense, but doesn't really.

Sometimes we can tell what is illogical or contradictory about a mixed message and sometimes we can't quite, but what we always know is that they *feel* wrong. The reason we send mixed messages is that the truth is inconvenient or unpleasant, and we hope to pull a fast one on the truth by our use of language. The reason we find mixed messages so unacceptable when we receive them is for exactly the same reason — the sender has played fast and loose with the truth.

Don't send mixed messages. Be braver than that and tell the truth. Don't accept mixed messages, either. Be smarter than that and ask for the truth.

WATCH OUT FOR HIDDEN AGENDAS —
FIRST OF ALL, IN YOURSELF.

TIP 7

FEEDBACK IS GREAT
WHEN IT ISN'T JUST
DISGUISED CRITICISM

You give feedback when you're worried that a person is doing something harmful to himself or herself or harmful to the family as a whole. Your motivation is love.

Criticism is something very different. Criticism comes from a place of anger, jealousy, vengeful feelings, regret — even from a place of self-hatred. You feel bad about yourself or your circumstances and you take it out on another person. The message you send is loaded with hate, and the person receiving the message knows that your intent is to hurt and punish.

If you want to say something about those fifteen pounds your son put on in the last few months, first get clear with yourself that your goal isn't to vent or to express your disgust or disappointment. Your goal is to wonder aloud with him if a way can be found to deal with the problem or whether those extra pounds are to be a part of his life now. You'll want to think about ways you can contribute to solving the problem before you bring the matter up. Also consider what you want to say, if anything, if he reacts defensively or doesn't perceive it as a problem at all.

The same is true if you want to give feedback about an alcohol problem, a school problem, or any habit or behavior that you think is harming one of your loved ones. You want to join with them, in words and in spirit, rather than point a finger and push them away. It's vital that you *do* give feedback, because there's no love without the courage to speak up about genuine problems. Silence is not a good or a loving response to problems. Keeping clear in your own mind the difference between feedback and criticism is the first step toward helping everybody in your family learn that a spirit of concern is welcome, but taking pot shots out of personal unhappiness isn't.

⊙

DON'T THROW STONES AT PEOPLE.
VERBAL ATTACKS
HURT AND PUT THE LIE TO YOUR
DECLARATIONS OF LOVE.

TIP 8

ALWAYS ASK FOR CLARIFICATION IF YOU DON'T UNDERSTAND

Often we don't understand what our mate, child, or sibling is saying to us. That may be because she is sending a mixed message, has a secret agenda, hasn't thought through what she is saying, is embarrassed by something that has happened, or is only communicating a small part of what is on her mind. This can be frustrating — until we remember that we can always ask questions! Nothing feels better than asking for clarification and discovering that a fear you were harboring was ungrounded. You just misunderstood what your mate, child, or sibling was saying.

Be careful when you ask for clarification, because our first impulse is to criticize the speaker for not being clear or to lash out because we didn't like the message we received. The most common response — "What did you mean by that?" — is often just an attack question and not a request for clarification at all. Its translation is "How dare you say that!" So, it is good to have some alternative ways to ask for clarification. All of the following are better than "What did you mean by that?"

- "I think you're saying _____, but I'm not positive. Am I close?"

- "There was a part there that I don't think I understood. What did you mean when you said _____?"

- "I'm a little confused. I think you said _____. But you also said

_____. Did I get that right?"

• "I think I understand what you're saying, but I'm not a hundred percent sure. Could you tell me a little more?"

Asking for clarification is an excellent communication skill that prevents small and large misunderstandings. If your daughter says, "My biology teacher is stupid," don't leap to the conclusion that your daughter is failing biology. Ask for clarification. She may only mean that in her opinion her biology teacher is stupid for giving so much home-work and so many pop quizzes, but that she plans to get even by getting an "A" in biology anyway. Wasn't that good to clear up?

©

ASK LOVING QUESTIONS. STAY IN
LOVING DIALOGUE UNTIL YOU UNDERSTAND.

TIP 9

DON'T LET STRESS DO THE TALKING

One of the biggest problems that families have in trying to communicate lovingly and effectively is that their stress gets in the way and does most or all of the talking.

People feel stressed and anxious a lot of the time. Mom is stressed by the demands of her job; Dad is stressed by the demands of his job; both are stressed by their commutes and money worries; the kids are stressed by school and stressed because mom and dad are stressed. Given this scenario, is it any wonder that angry outbursts often make up so large a part of family communications?

Try not to let stress do the talking. Instead, use this approach to create patient interchanges:

- Think before you speak
- Speak from love, not irritation
- Be empathic and care about your listener
- Admit to being stressed
- Reduce the stress in your life

Learn a few stress reduction and anxiety management techniques as soon as you can. There are plenty of books and tapes that can help you. Give them a try!

⊚

BEFORE YOU SPEAK, WATCH OUT FOR
STRESS AND ANXIETY.
THEY ARE THE SILENT KILLERS OF
COMMUNICATION.

TIP 10

SPEAK TO CORE VALUES AND LET THE LITTLE THINGS SLIDE

If you're looking for interpersonal problems, you'll find them everywhere. You could spend your whole life upset about your husband's unwillingness to help with the gardening, your wife's small anxiety attacks when company is due, your sister's way of "borrowing" your CDs, or your dad's temper tantrums when you don't get your chores done.

It doesn't pay to sweat the small things. On the other hand, it is vital that you speak when your core values *are* involved. Do you know what your core values are? One might be that you refuse to be verbally abused (or abused in any way). If and when that happens, you need to speak up immediately. Another might be that you don't want to be made to feel small or worthless. A third might be that you don't want to be lied to about anything important. Take some time right now to make a list of your core values.

Sometimes we think that our core values are involved in some interaction because of the way we construct our inner language. When a chore doesn't get done we may feel "betrayed," because inside we're saying "If they loved me they would pick up after themselves. They must not care about me at all!" That the chores aren't getting done is a problem, but speaking to yourself this way is a *bigger* problem, because it leads to a sense of catastrophe where only a midsized problem exists. Be sure that your core values really have been violated *before* you speak, but if they have been, then make sure that you *do* speak.

◎

PICK YOUR BATTLES. ONLY FIGHT
WHEN A CORE VALUE IS AT STAKE.

TIP 11

GIVE EVERYBODY A CHANCE TO SPEAK

Sometimes family members don't feel that it is safe or wise to speak. Maybe your youngest child feels that what she has to say is never taken seriously, or maybe Dad feels that he can't talk as articulately as other family members. For a family to work, everyone's voice needs to be heard. Using the following suggestions will help give everybody in your family a chance to speak.

If it is a family issue — say, where you are going to spend your summer vacation — ask everyone to write down his or her ideas on a single sheet of paper. Then give everybody copies of all the sheets of paper and time to think about them. Call a family meeting for that evening or the next day and make sure that everybody's ideas are treated respectfully. If someone isn't speaking, ask that person for his or her thoughts and feelings. It may be that the final decision rests with Mom and Dad, but it's still empowering to feel that you have had your say. It's doubly empowering if what you've said is taken seriously and affects the outcome.

Watch out for who's being cut off. If Rebecca is always cutting off her younger sister Louise, say, "Rebecca, Louise gets a chance to complete her sentences and her thoughts. She'll tell you when she's finished." If you find your mate hasn't the patience to hear what you have to say and cuts you off, object lovingly but firmly. "I need to be able to finish my thoughts, love. Try to be patient."

Occasionally ask yourself, "Does it feel like

everybody in this household is being heard? Or are some voices dominating?" If any voices are being silenced or left out, make a pact with yourself to do something to change that family dynamic.

◎

EVERYBODY HAS A VOICE.
EVERYBODY NEEDS TO SPEAK
AND BE HEARD.

TIP 12

TALK ABOUT SHARING — INCLUDING SHARING THE POWER

Families ought to be the place where the most sharing occurs. Too often they aren't. Dad, who can't control much at work, wants to come home and at least control the dinner hour and the decibel levels around him. He doesn't want to discuss and negotiate. Mom, whose job may be just as stressful as Dad's, and who has the added burden of making dinner, expects her requests to be honored without debate. She too hasn't an ounce of energy left to deal with whining and complaints. Ideals of sharing go by the board as family members attempt to control whatever they can.

Sharing the power, control, and authority is still the best and most loving way to operate. Family members who act responsibly, whether they're six or ninety, should get to exert their fair share of control and have something to say about things like bed times, spending habits, lunch desires, television viewing, and even the most important things, like how they want to be treated and addressed.

Sharing also means that when a decision affects the whole family, everybody's needs get taken seriously. If you know that you have to move from San Francisco to Atlanta and that the children have no say in the matter, you can still share the power by inviting them to have meaningful input into significant aspects of the move: such as, where in Atlanta they might like to live. You could view homes for sale on the internet as a family or even make a family visit to Atlanta. If you open your heart and mind to the fact that the children have a stake in this move, you may end up relinquishing some control but investing in their self-esteem and happiness.

⊚

SHare everyTHING — THe Love,
THe LaUGHTer, THe Tears
... anD THe reINS.

TIP 13

PRESENT BIG NEWS CAREFULLY AND COMPLETELY

Many times people don't want to talk about unpleasant things, even if — and sometimes because — they're the most important things. Parents don't want to let their kids know about a cancer diagnosis, admit that they've lost their job, . . . that they're being transferred. Kids don't want to confess to their parents that they're pregnant, failing at college, or being bullied at school. No one may want to confront that major family upheaval — the divorce. It is far better to present such life-shaking news than to keep it hidden, because presenting it gives family members the chance to pull together, lend a hand, and meet the challenge.

BaD NeWS IS FaMILY NeWS.
LeT PEOPLe KNOW — aND
LeT THEM HELP!

TIP 14

TROUBLESHOOT FAMILY FEARS

Many people fear flying, spiders, public speaking, intruders, losing their job, contracting diseases, driving at night, even going shopping or just going out. When these fears are severe, we call them phobias. Millions of people suffer from phobias and other anxiety disorders, and everyone is anxious or afraid some of the time. When people are afraid, they find it nearly impossible to communicate.

What rarely helps is to say to someone who is

anxious or afraid "Don't worry" or "There is nothing to fear." Here are some communication tips that do work:

- "Is there anything I can do to help?"
- "I know it feels really scary to do
  _____, but I wonder if it would be possible to do _____ at least?"
- "Would it help if we talked about it?"
- "Do you know what scares me? _____.
  Here's what I've learned to do that helps
  a little."

Many difficult family situations occur because someone is afraid of something and doesn't want to communicate that fact to anyone else. Jennifer, for all her bravado, may actually be afraid of getting behind the wheel for the first time. Johnny may be afraid that his grades have fallen just enough that he's ruined his chances of getting into his first choice college. Mom may be afraid that her job is really too taxing and is harming her health and even more frightened about thinking about a job search or a career change. Dad may be afraid that his failure to plan for retirement means that he'll have to keep working forever. These fears affect family life tremendously, and yet they are among the hardest things for people — even those who love each other dearly — to talk about.

Talking about them *helps.* Airing your fears is always a winning idea.

WHEN YOU'RE AFRAID, SAY SO.
THAT'S REAL COURAGE.

TIP 15

PLAN FOR TOGETHERNESS BUT ALLOW FOR PRIVACY

Many families demand togetherness, even when everyone in the family knows beforehand that the experience will be a miserable one.

Often there seem to be excellent reasons for this forced togetherness: a family dinner could allow for folks to check in, a family vacation could allow for quality time together, and so on. At an intellectual level, this is true. But at an emotional level, forced togetherness can be a straitjacket that brings out the worst in people.

Spontaneous gatherings are almost always better than forced gatherings. Spontaneous gatherings are full of love, laughter, and good feelings. When everyone *wants* to watch the same video, and then someone gets the urge to make popcorn, and then someone else gets it into his head to make lemonade, a real family party with real heart and togetherness erupts. These are the events that people remember for a lifetime.

If the scales have to be tipped one way or the

other, tip them in favor of allowing family members their private moments. A family shouldn't feel like a prison, and family members shouldn't feel like prisoners. Enjoy your time together and by all means do plan for togetherness, but in human-sized chunks: special dinners rather than every dinner, or one-day outings rather than whole weeks together in a pint-sized cabin. By moderating your demand for togetherness, you support and honor everybody's need for privacy.

◎

TOGETHERNESS IS A BLESSING,
BUT SO IS PRIVACY.

TIP 16

TRUST YOUR INTUITION THAT THERE IS A PROBLEM

When you have an intuition that a problem exists — that your son is in trouble, that your husband is angry with you, that your sister is having a crisis — you shouldn't ignore that feeling. Almost always that intuition is right on the money. Stop everything and chat with yourself about what you think might be going on. "What's up with Bill? I know he's angry with me. Was it that silly little thing I said at dinner? Or is he still stewing about my decision to visit my parents at Thanksgiving? No...it doesn't feel like either of those. I guess I have no idea."

Then check in with him. Of course that may feel hard to do, because you might get into an argument or have to defend yourself against his charges. Relationships that can't stand up to the airing of disagreements are on shaky ground already, and talking about them is always better than letting things fester. Trust your intuition that something is up, take time to think through what that might be, prepare yourself as best you can, and then courageously say,

"I *know* you're angry with me about something. Can we talk?"

◎

YOUR INTUITION IS A GIFT. BE AS RESPONSIVE TO IT AS YOU WOULD BE TO A CANARY CHIRPING AWAY IN A MINE TUNNEL.

TIP 17

SAY "PLEASE" WHEN
YOU MEAN IT
AND "THANK YOU"
ALL THE TIME

Often we say please when we don't mean it. We say "Please mow the lawn today" or "Please bring down your laundry" when in fact we mean "You'd better mow the lawn today or I'll be angry with you" or "Haven't you learned by now that I need all the laundry down here first thing Sunday morning?"

Please means "It would please me." If you really mean "It would please me if you would bring down the laundry, but of course you get to decide based on what's going on in your life," then by all means use please in that sentence. But if your son replies, "It would please me if I stayed in bed two more hours, rather than bringing down the laundry," you'll just have to laugh and say to yourself, "Well, that's what I get for giving him options!"

Please is not a command word. It is a request word. It means that the person you're talking to has the option of saying no. Sometimes we think that if we say "please" the other person is obliged to say "yes." That isn't so. Requests are requests and demands are demands and never the twain shall meet. When you are making a request, by all means use "please." When you are making a demand or a declaration, choose some other form of speech, like "Bring down your laundry in the next fifteen minutes if you want me to wash your gym clothes for Monday."

Thank you is *very* different. You can't say "thank you" too much. "Thank you! It's great to have you for a son!" "Thank you, Mom! I really appreciated that!" No, you can't say "thank you" too often. *Please* is a tricky little word, but *thank you* is as good as a phrase gets.

©

EXPRESS GRATITUDE! SAY "THANK YOU."

TIP 18

IF SOMEONE ISN'T
COOPERATING,
USE LOVE AND
CONSEQUENCES

You've just caught your teenage son smoking. You're sad, angry, upset, and scared to death, and your first impulse is to wring his neck. Try leading with love instead. At the same time, let him know that actions have consequences. Your message might sound like this:

"I love you very much, but I need you to stop smoking. I know that now that you've begun it may be very hard — even incredibly hard — to get you to stop, and I'm going to need to take some serious steps to reverse this. To begin with I'm going to enroll you in a smoke-ending program, ground you, and I don't know what else."

Let him know what the consequences will be if he continues smoking. The second half of your speech might sound like this: "If I learn that you're still smoking, you can't do any extracurricular activities this year. And let's not even talk about driving! I love you too much to stand by and watch you cut short your life by ten or twenty years."

@

CONSEQUENCES WITHOUT LOVE
are JUST PUNISHMENTS.

TIP 19

ALLOW FOR GROWTH
AND CHANGE —
IN FACT, ENCOURAGE
THEM

Children grow and change. That is as it should be. Adults also grow and change, if they are lucky. They acquire some better ideas of what they want to achieve and contribute. They learn to let go of stress and anger. They live more in the moment. They express their love more easily and more often. They communicate better.

Encourage growth and change by the language you use and the messages you send. Say, "I think you've been making some terrific changes! I'm impressed!"

Praise positive change and praise the natural milestones of growth, like riding a two-wheeler and surviving the prom. Become a cheerleader for all the positive changes you and your family have it in you to make.

TELL THE ONES YOU LOVE HOW
WELL THEY ARE DOING!

TIP 20

practice communication skills daily

reat athletes practice. Great singers practice. Great pianists practice. Great communicators also practice.

Consciously create opportunities to communicate. Brew a pot of tea and ask your mate, "Shall we check in?" Visit your daughter at bedtime and say, "We haven't talked for weeks about that problem at school. How's it been going?" If she replies, "Fine," go the next step. "That's great! How'd it resolve itself?" If she stops you with "I don't want to talk about it," get very serious and very loving and say, "Sweetheart, that's okay, but I'll be in my room reading if you want to check in about it." Leave your heart and your door open.

Practice your communication skills. You'll be amazed. You'll actually know what your mate and your children are thinking and feeling. You'll feel connected to everyone in your family, and they'll feel connected to you. When problems arise, you'll be expert at finding the best solutions. There's no greater love you can offer your family than communicating well and inviting them to communicate well in return.

◎

HAVE REAL CONVERSATIONS WITH YOUR
LOVED ONES — EVERY DAY.

☙ AFTERWORD ☙

This has been a brief look at better family communications. Other volumes in this series may also be of help to you. Keep your eyes peeled for them!

I'd like to leave you with a final thought. It pays to paint a mind picture of what might be. Athletes, performers, salespeople, and folks in many walks of life are taught to visualize success. You should, too, because visualization is really affirmation. If you can picture you and your mate, you and your child, or you and your sibling in intimate conversation, each listening well and speaking from the heart, each sharing thoughts and feelings, you're also affirming the possibility that this can and will happen. And it can! With practice, patience, and cooperation you and your loved ones can launch a new era of family harmony and togetherness.

I hope this book has encouraged you and I wish you the best of luck in your coming communication adventures!

◎

Create Your Own Family's
Communication Tips

TIP 1 _____

_____

TIP 2 _____

_____

TIP 3 _____

_____

TP 4 _____

_____

TP 5 _____

_____

TP 6 _____

_____

TP 7 _____

_____

⊚ ABOUT THE AUTHOR ⊚

Eric Maisel, Ph.D., is a licensed marriage and family therapist, national certified counselor, and faculty member of St. Mary's College (Moraga, California). In addition to his counseling work with individuals, couples, and families, Dr. Maisel is a nationally known creativity consultant whose books include:

Fearless Creating
A Life in the Arts

Deep Writing

Affirmations for Artists

Fearless Presenting

Lving the Writer's Life

Sleep Thinking

The Creativity Book

He has also contributed to New World Library's *The Soul of Creativity* and written for many periodicals, among them *Writer's Digest, Dramatics Magazine,* and *Intuition Magazine.*

Dr. Maisel lives in Concord, California, with his

wife Ann Mathesius Maisel, Assistant Head of Lick-Wilmerding High School in San Francisco, and their youngest daughter, Kira, a sophomore in high school. Their eldest daughter, Natalya, is a student at the University of California at Berkeley, and Dr. Maisel's son by his first marriage, David, lives in Amsterdam, where he works in cyberspace and flies small planes in actual space. The Maisels also have four cats: Max, Sam, Charlie, and Bailey.

Dr. Maisel is available to speak about family communication problems and solutions. He would also love to hear from readers about their communication successes, challenges, or anything else they'd like to share. He can be reached in the following ways:

Eric Maisel, Ph.D.
P. O. Box 613 • Concord, CA 94522-0613
Office Phone: (925) 689-0210
Fax: (925) 689-0210
Email: amaisel@sirius.com
http://www.ericmaisel.com